About the Author

Pete Burgess was born in Crewe, Cheshire. He developed an ability to produce witty poems for colleagues and friends during a long career in IT. Pete's first book of poetry reflects his time at Edleston Road Primary school built in 1875 and affectionately known to this day as "Eggy Road".

Eggy Road

Poems from a Sixties schoolkid

Pete Burgess

Apart from any fair dealing for the purposes of research or private study,
or criticism or review, as permitted under the Copyright, Designs and Patents
Act 1988, this publication may only be reproduced, stored or transmitted, in
any form or by any means, with the prior permission in writing of the
publishers, or in the case of reprographic reproduction in accordance with
the terms of licences issued by the Copyright Licensing Agency. Enquiries
concerning reproduction outside those terms should be sent to the publishers.

Matador
Unit E2 Airfield Business Park,
Harrison Road, Market Harborough,
Leicestershire. LE16 7UL
Tel: 0116 2792299
Email: books@troubador.co.uk
Web: www.troubador.co.uk/matador
Twitter: @matadorbooks

ISBN 978 1803130 286

British Library Cataloguing in Publication Data.
A catalogue record for this book is available from the British Library.

Printed and bound in Great Britain by 4edge Limited
Typeset in 11pt Adobe Garamond Pro by Troubador Publishing Ltd, Leicester, UK

Matador is an imprint of Troubador Publishing Ltd

To Jan, Craig, Lee & Anthony

Contents

First Day   1

Staff Room   3

Tuck Shop   4

Milk Monitor   5

Traded but Faded   7

New Kit   8

Dog in the Playground   9

School Dinners   11

Swimming   12

Hidden Skills!   14

Whatever Happened to Duffle Bags?   15

Nit Nurse   16

Accessorised   17

Dear Santa…   18

Knitted Goods   19

Ice-Ice Maybe   20

Recorders   21

Tony Grazier's Brother   22

Bruises   23

Cycling Proficiency Test   24

The Fountain of Youth   25

The Green Mile   27

Swot	29
Conkers	31
Casey	33
An Ode to Gerry Anderson	34
Wayfinders	35
Marbles	37
Elasticity	39
Fan-Gas-Tic	41
I Never Heard the Car…	43
Teacher's Pet	45
Jack & Phil	47
Contents of a Small Boy's Satchel	48
Inventory of a Small Boy's Satchel	50
Half-Term	51
Lost Property	52
He-Said-She-Said	53
Confiscation	56
Kathy Won't Be In Today	57
My Goal	59
Handstands	61
LSD (aka Pounds Shillings and Pence)	63
School Trip	65
Frogspawn	66
Eleven-Plus	68
Class Sharpener	70
Blue Peter Badge	71
Puddles	73
That's Entertainment	74

First Day

The summer's almost over, and my world's been just play,
But September's leaves are changing – as my life from today,
I've swapped my clothes for uniform, it doesn't feel quite right,
My mum made sure I washed myself and had an early night.

I know where I am going to – I've passed it many times,
It's big it's brick, it echoes with the sound of playground rhymes,
I've never stepped inside it though and time is drawing near,
My stomach has a knot in it, I can't hold back a tear.

My mum has reassured me that there's nothing here to dread,
That's not what I've been feeling since my early trip to bed.
Everyone's a giant and they know just what to do,
I'll never find my way around I haven't got a clue.

I grip Mum's hand more tightly and huddle to her side,
With one foot on another I try to shrink and hide.
She stoops to reassure me, and neatens up my clothes,
Just then a giant comes in sight and strikes a fearful pose.

She swings her arm – I hear a bell, the clock has just struck nine,
The playground now falls silent as the giants fall in line.
A hundred mummy's soldiers march off to classroom spaces,
Leaving just some four-year-olds with startled little faces.

I'm not the only midget left – there's lots of us around,
And better still, I know a few – some kindred spirits found!
The giant with the fearsome bell now smiles and looks our way,
She's talking to assembled mums about this fearful day.

Too soon the grips are loosened, and we're ushered to a door,
Last minute hugs and kisses given just to reassure.
We follow like a gingham snake unable to resist.
And soon we have forgotten all the reasons we were kissed.

We have a hook to hang our coats, our name is on each one,
There's toys and milk and chairs and books, there's some for everyone.
My senses fill with all that's new – the sights, the smells, the sounds,
I don't know where to turn my head – imagination bounds.
No longer thinking of my mum, I hang my bag and coat,
My days of play are over and never more remote.

Staff Room

I pass it daily, skipping gaily never looking in,
It's just a door, it's nothing more I've never been within.
But just inside, the giants hide, the only ones allowed,
They drink and smoke and tell a joke – with voices deep and loud.

I'm curious like all of us and wonder what they plot,
Venetian blinds hide all their kind – I wonder what they've got?
Will we find out, and ease our doubt of what the teachers do?
The only way we'll plan someday to take a peek or two.

I'll pass the door – it is no more, I've more important work,
My bum's been pinched, it's made me flinch – and made me go berserk.
I turn to run and find the one – I'm fairly sure I know,
I'll leave the room and plans of doom there's always tomorrow!

Tuck Shop

I've threepence in my pocket it's earmarked for some treats,
I've got to get it out of there – invest it in some sweets.
The tuck shop has the options for a buyer such as me,
The problem is just what to choose when finally, it's three.

The clock hands move so slowly but at last the schoolday's done,
I grab my coat and satchel and break into a run.
Look left look right and left again then dash across the street,
I turn the shop door handle and my day's about complete!

There's pick-and-mix and sherbet dips, fruit salads and white mice,
There's kola cubes and fizz in tubes and sugared puffed up rice.
I calculate my options looking for the best return,
If only I had sixpence! That amount I too could burn.

But threepence is my limit and I've worked it to the max,
A bag is filled with tiny sweets in multicoloured packs.
I've Parma violets, love hearts, fruit salads and some jellies
Not what a nutritionist would advise for little bellies!

Milk Monitor

With every term there came a chance to miss a bit of class,
It came if chosen to deliver cow juice cased in glass,
Milk Monitor was the job title, to donate without prescription,
"A third of a pint to everyone" the only job description.

So, when the local dairyman electrically supplied,
We'd rush out to the tower of crates to do our job with pride,
Twenty-eight for Mr Dixon, the same for Mrs Leeds,
Thirty-six for Mr Christie (they'll need it – they're all weeds).

There's a wobble on the trolley, a stubborn wheel or two,
The sound of clinking glass on metal forms an entry cue,
No one had lactose issues, no soya and no skimmed,
Just pasteurised for everyone, in a bottle, silver rimmed.

Unless of course it's Christmas, when things got somewhat jolly,
And we got golden bottle tops with berries and green holly,
And just to make things different we got some bottled squash,
The brand was "Suki Suncap" and it gave us sugar rush.

The job itself was payless but it did have perks to use,
As any milk left over was the monitor's to refuse,
It was great when it was summer and the milk was still quite cool,
But in winter radiators used to defrost the dairy fuel.

This meant that sometimes pupils had a playtime treat in store,
As the thawing of the milk pushed out a creamy frozen core.
"Ice cream" they'd shout and quickly take their bottle from the heat,
Whilst we the unpaid monitors waited for the spares to eat.

Traded but Faded

The coalman delivered with a beaming white grin,
The sweep kept the chimney clean with brush from within,
The Corona man brought all the pop we could drink,
Whilst dawn saw the milkman with bottles that chinked,
The man from the Pru collected cash for our future,
And don't forget bike-pedalled goods from the butcher,
The visiting nurse tended our bumps and our rashes,
The dustman worked hard to get rid of our ashes,
We read from the papers delivered by youth,
And paid bob a job to help fix the Cubs' roof,
Shopping from home was via Freemans or Kays,
The chippy, the only source of our take-away,
Our unwanted goods were classed rag & bone,
Collected on a cart by a man on his own,
Our toiletries supplied by a lady from Avon,
With choices for all with prices we'd save on,
Most now have gone, their fate has been met,
As we turn to our phones and click on the Net.

New Kit

It's games today, more time to play!
I've got my pump bag – see it sway?
The lesson seems too far away,
I wish it would come faster.

Mum packed my kit, yes all of it,
With name tags sewn on every bit!
If something's lost, she'll have a fit!
(I'd better check it after.)

I've tried it on – it's all too long!
How could she get my size so wrong?
And when the others come along,
I'll bet they'll laugh and taunt me.

But at PE they're just like me,
With shorts hung lower than their knee,
Mums know it's part of history,
That we'll all fit in it shortly.

Dog in the Playground

We've had assembly, said our prayers,
We've trudged to class up well-worn stairs,
And now it's time for lungs to air,
As morning playtime beckons.

The bell rings once and we're let out,
To a place where we can scream and shout,
But what's that darting in and out?
A dog's got in I reckon.

No games for now we all agree,
We've got to stop this canine spree,
The dog displays four-legged glee,
As we descend upon it.

An age flies by but in the end,
The dog is cornered by a friend,
A fingered collar signals the end,
As Fido is defeated.

Some scruffy mongrel now and then,
Would somehow manage to get in,
With wagging tail and toothy grin
Would run to whom it's owned.

If that should happen then there'd be,
A moment of celebrity,
For dog and owner equally,
And time off to take it home!

School Dinners

One hour thirty, hands not dirty,
Time to feed our hungry party,
The dinner queue was always chirpy,
A hundred pupils long.

Walk in couples never troubled,
Teachers had their portions doubled,
Vats of yellow custard bubbled,
As infant chatter rang.

Smiling faces saying Graces,
Stepped on someone's untied laces,
Uniform with gravy traces,
Before we finish firsts.

Little speakers, thirsty features,
Multicoloured plastic beakers,
Water was all they would give us,
Enough for all our thirsts.

Swimming

Every Monday after school,
You'd see me scowl,
With trunks and towel.
Following the unwritten rule
Of learning not to drown

Off to a building council owned,
Chlorine fumes,
And dressing rooms.
Behind whose doors we'd get unrobed
We'd shiver and we'd frown.

Blue rectangles met us there,
White tiles all round,
An echoing sound.
Instructor with a float to spare
For those who couldn't swim

A smaller pool kept extra warm,
To coax you in,
To make you grin,
You could reach the bottom with your arm,
Your nostrils filled with Vim.

Progression obvious to all,
With floats then bands,
Then legs and hands,
No frisbee or a coloured ball,
Just float then kick then stroke.

Would Mondays always end this way?
Then came the session,
The final lesson,
I heard the swim instructor say,
"A width please – and don't choke."

An empty pool, except for me,
A width she said,
I'll end up dead!
I think I need another wee,
Before I take the test.

A whistle shrieked and off I sped,
Arms were flailing,
Legs just trailing,
Water just below my head,
But swimming yes – at last!

Hidden Skills!

I once knew a boy named Lawrence,
Who was able to swear – and in torrents!
Things starting with B and with F and with C,
And much more should the need ever warrant.

His skill was only uncovered,
When he became overly bothered,
Then he'd shout and he'd curse,
With no need to rehearse
(All out of the earshot of mother) …

Whatever Happened to Duffle Bags?

Whatever happened to duffle bags? That once were used by all,
They didn't have a brand name – well not as I recall.
I can't remember Nike staring at me from one ever,
Puma and Adidas were just names I'd heard of – never.
They were practical and spacious with not a zip in sight,
They had a bit of string attached to close the neck up tight.
You could use them for PE kit or for your trunks and towel,
You could even Pac-a-mac inside when weather turned out foul.
Compare it with almost any bag – I think that it did match all.
But just for looks and holding books – think I'd keep my satchel!

Nit Nurse

Each year at beginning of term,
Our heads would be checked to confirm,
That when thoroughly tested,
Our scalps weren't infested,
With friends we'd wish not to return.

A comb was the tool she'd prefer,
Minute little prongs through the hair,
If bugs came a-rustling,
Shampoo so disgusting,
Was prescribed to red-faced parents there.

Accessorised

To make a five-year-old look neat,
From head to waist from leg to feet,
The only thing a mum would need,
The Market could supply.

It sold for pennies nothing more,
Cheaper than the local store,
It would wash and wash for evermore,
On that you could rely.

It could be thin it could be fat,
Invariably it was flat,
A knot or stitch and that was that,
And ready to be worn.

So, round the sock just at the top,
In skirts to stop them from the drop,
To tame the most unruly mop,
Elastic was the norm.

Dear Santa...

Stickle bricks or Lego,
Perhaps it was Meccano,
Railway sets by Triang made us sigh,
Sheriff badge and matching hats,
Cowboy guns that fired caps,
An Action Man complete with moving eyes.

An orange Raleigh Chopper,
Or inflatable space hopper,
And don't forget the range of Matchbox cars,
An Airfix ship to build,
A Stylophone that trilled,
Selection box from Cadbury or Mars.

The ultimate selection,
For any boy's collection,
Was none of the above (or so I've heard),
An eight-year-old's idea of heaven,
Was a gun called Johnny Seven,
Or a clockwork sparking model Thunderbird.

Knitted Goods

My Nan knit me a jumper I'm wearing it to school,
I'll take it off at playtime – I don't think it looks cool,
She knit a pair of gloves as well, one's loose and one is tight,
The left one's got 4 fingers but there's 6 upon the right.
She's knit a woolly hat for me I'm worried by the size,
I'm sure it's not supposed to need holes cut out for my eyes!
The scarf is better though I think my neck will never freeze,
She said in just a year or so it won't hang round my knees.
She's going to knit me something else and asked me what I'd like,
I thought I might be pushing it if I asked her for a bike.

Ice-Ice Maybe

In winter it was always nice,
To make a slide upon the ice.

The playground was the place to be,
While teachers drank their morning tea.

The boys would find the deepest snow,
And trample it with heel and toe.

Until it shone so smooth and straight,
While a queue of children lay in wait.

Fifteen minutes slippery fun,
For shrieking kids in winter sun.

Some would slide and some would trip,
An elbow banged, an injured hip.

Then back to class with smiles so wide,
From spending break time on the slide.

Eager for the lunchtime thrill,
Where all could sharpen up their skill.

A repeat performance usually damned,
By a caretaker with a shovel of sand!

Recorders

We all had to learn the recorder,
No choice, it was headmaster's order,
They were plastic or wooden,
No such thing as a good 'un,
It sounded like cats being murdered.

Tony Grazier's Brother

Tony Grazier's elder brother was unlike any other,
He could whistle with his fingers in his mouth,
When I asked could he show me, he frowned at brother Tony,
And said we were too young and couldn't pout.

I said to Tony's brother that me and just one other,
Would keep his secret if he'd show us how.
He grinned and said it just won't happen, until you fill that gap in,
Between those baby teeth inside your mouths.

Bruises

One thing for sure that we all shared,
Was every time our limbs were bared,
You'd see a range of coloured patterns,
Each told a story of how it happened.

A hematoma of the tissue,
They came and went without an issue,
A badge of honour from a fall,
Resulting from a game of ball.

A tumble from an early cycle,
A clumsy lunge from a netball rival,
Would raise a lump of colour red,
Which changed in days to purple instead.

They'd change again with yellow hues,
Their cause becoming yesterday's news,
Even when they made us sore,
Most never worried about their cause.

But some held secrets for the bearer,
Anger from their family carer?
Hidden anguish if truth were told,
Affected futures to unfold.

Cycling Proficiency Test

Fifteen volunteers, all ears,
15 pairs of wheels, and fears,
30 little eyes, some tears,
Will they see it through?

Playground changed, it looks strange,
Traffic cones, a massive range!
Hope somebody will explain,
Just what we'll have to do.

One at a time, all in line,
Before we start, we look behind,
Not too fast, we're doing fine,
As we begin the test.

Keeping straight, a steady rate,
Before we turn, apply the brake,
Make the signals – no mistake,
We're feeling less distressed.

Two hours passed, gone so fast!
Learnt some skills – I hope they last,
Earned my badge and haven't crashed,
On my cycling proficiency test.

The Fountain of Youth

There's seven on the mission and we've got a competition,
The time is set for break time after lunch,
We're drinking water with passion like it's going out of fashion,
We really are a dedicated bunch.

With beaker after beaker drunk quickly behind teacher,
Water swashing down our little throats,
The plan swings into motion and there may be some commotion,
When the bell rings and we head out in our coats.

But the clock just isn't moving, our situation's not improving,
There's still ten minutes left before we're free,
The water has stopped swilling as our bladders started filling,
Now everybody feels in agony.

At last, the bell is ringing, and the doors are quickly flinging,
We dash out to the place where bikes are parked,
In break time after dinner it's time to find a winner,
The one who truly plans to leave his mark.

So, seven little nippers pull seven little zippers,
A widened smile descends upon them all,
As water gulped before hits the gulley in the floor,
And then is aimed expertly up the wall.

There was a target mark, identified by chalk,
That proudly showed the record reached to date,
But despite an aim for Heaven not even one of seven,
Could match the effort by their closest mate.

So back to final classes the disappointed masses,
Left wondering how they could take the crown,
The mate they had just greeted told them he had cheated,
And revealed the water pistol he had found…

The Green Mile

Tarmac was fine for playtime,
It did for twenty minutes,
But as we got near nine or ten,
We knew it had its limits.

Our limbs were getting stronger,
And we all were growing fast,
So, when time came to do PE,
The playground wasn't tasked.

Our school had an arrangement,
(As did others from around),
To use a field on Gresty Road,
Just past the Alex's ground.

We'd assemble with our kit bags,
And pick a partner all,
Then walk the mile, a crocodile,
For games with bat and ball.

For girls it would be rounders,
Or skipping with a rope,
For boys it would be soccer,
(Not cricket we'd all hope).

We'd walk there in all weathers,
We'd play in rain or shine,
A patch of green for Townies,
An hour at a time.

The changing room was wooden,
And doubled as a store,
If anyone forgot the key,
We just got changed outdoors.

No showers when we finished,
Or heating when times were cold,
We never needed stuff like that,
At nearly ten years old.

Some nine or ten years after,
They'd sold the patch of green,
To a property developer,
For a figure quite obscene.

It's now a sea of houses,
Identical in style,
No hut, no grass, no football nets,
Just brick, cement, and tile.

Swot

I wasn't good at doing sums,
My spelling wasn't great,
I never put my hand up,
And my homework had mistakes.

When others got a gold star,
Mine would just be red,
I'd have settled for a silver,
If the truth were to be said.

But now there are improvements,
My marks are on the up,
A lot more ticks than crosses,
Are appearing in my book.

My arithmetic is mental,
My words are all correct,
I even know some capitals,
And no one yet suspects.

I've got myself an ally,
She now sits next to me,
I kissed her in the playground,
Now I get stuff for free!

Her book is always open,
She whispers in my ear,
I meet her at the tuck shop,
When homework time is near.

Good things don't last forever,
And this is just the same,
My marks will soon go downward,
When I'm put in the frame.

You see she thinks I love her,
But that was just last week,
Her best friend has a puppy,
And I'm going there for tea.

Conkers

August's leaves on heavy trees,
A harvest lies in wait,
Round and spiked, a sheer delight,
For any boy aged eight.

A special tree for boys like me,
Our bikes left on the ground,
Heads look up to view the crop,
Like treasure that's been found.

Jagged leaves with seven teeth,
Amass around its boughs,
Its spikey fruit we seek as loot,
If we hit them with our throws.

A heavy stick will do the trick,
As long as it's thrown true,
From three 'til dusk we aim for husks,
We need more than a few.

Arms grown tired and sticks expired,
Our bounty is complete,
A jagged mass of leaves on grass,
Is left around our feet.

Now the task the spikes unmask,
Our mission near fulfilled,
Smooth and brown with lighter crown,
And ready to be drilled.

Crown to base an old shoelace,
Is threaded through each bore,
Our ammunition, our next days' mission,
A morning play times' war.

Warring twos and waiting queues,
Are spread across the yard,
A string held tight, as fruits collide,
Some win and most will lose.

A playground strewn with chestnut spume,
Is all that's left behind,
A new top score at ten wins more,
This conker's hard as iron!

Casey

A football was known as a Casey,
It was heavy and tied up with laces,
And when it got wet,
Your life you could bet,
You could kick it no more than four paces.

Real leather was on the outside,
A rubber balloon filled the hide,
You'd knew if it once,
Hit you hard on the bonce,
It probably would make you cry.

The colour was orange or white,
Eighteen oblong panels stitched tight,
Each boy that would kick it,
Or head it or flick it,
Would long to keep it for the night!

An Ode to Gerry Anderson

We didn't worship astronauts or stars of aviation,
We didn't know he was birth of Supermarionation,
But still we tuned in every week with avid fascination,
To watch his puppets foil the plots of every alien nation.

His creations were fantastic, they defied all physics laws,
A Supercar with tiny wings could dive as well as soar,
The engines in a Thunderbird would heave a mighty roar,
And take off from an island ramp ascending from the floor.

The Titans never stood a chance Troy Tempest saw to that,
He'd blow them all to kingdom come and never lose his hat,
Drums would sound and suddenly Marineville would go flat,
Commander Shore would call the shots from anywhere he sat.

Steve Zodiac had orders to preserve all human life,
He did it with aplomb aboard his Fireball XL5,
In situations hopeless he still seemed to survive,
With a robot and an alien pet assembled in his tribe.

Now all you get is CGI or something from Japan,
Nothing yet has matched the skill bestowed upon that man,
I'm proud to say that I have been a puppet master's fan,
There are no strings on you, our hero, Gerry Anderson!

Wayfinders

My shoes were scuffed and seen much better days,
The tarmac wear had turned them black to grey.

So now was time to change for something new,
It was then that something novel came to view.

What was being worn by Cub Scout friends,
Had set all eight-year-olds a brand-new trend.

The media had already gone to town,
And a sixties footwear legend had been born.

Squared and black they didn't look unique,
But they were quite different underneath.

The soles had tracks of animals embossed,
And a compass – so you never could get lost.

What more could any eight-year-old desire,
With benefits all parents must require.

Made in England too as you could see,
By Bata in a place called Tilbury.

It couldn't now be Start-Rite or from Clarks,
And there was nothing like them sold in Marks.

The prices were no different we'd plead,
A pair of Wayfinders were all we'd ever need.

But just the same as any other fad,
They weren't the best footwear I'd ever had.

The compass hurt and broke within a week,
And all the tracks wore off beneath my feet.

But still a legend deep in children's minds,
For anyone whose now 'round sixty-five.

They were the shoes to have I can attest,
(Apart from football boots signed by Georgie Best)!

Marbles

If it wasn't raining,
And snow was not about,
You'd hear a line of boys and girls shout "Ringer" when let out.

This wasn't meant in malice,
Nor was it meant in hate,
It simply was to signify a game was to be played.

That game was played with marbles,
and Ringer was its name,
For certain of the players, it became their claim to fame.

One such was called Dave Manley,
Who had a useful dad,
His shooters were ball bearings from all the trucks he'd had.

And unbeknown to most kids,
Who'd played it just the once,
The odds were stacked against them as Dave's dad was no dunce.

He knew that a ball bearing,
Was identical in size,
But unlike one produced in glass it was heavier by miles.

So, each and every newbie,
Who knuckled down to play,
Would end up losing marbles in a very subtle way.

The bearing didn't roll much,
On a lumpy tarmac floor,
So, Dave just made a killing as the others failed to score.

He'd never lose his bearing,
As it stopped near on command,
Whilst all the others' shooters went careering past – as planned!

So, Dave became a legend,
Unworthy you might feel,
But everybody knew him as "Manley – balls of steel!"

Elasticity

We talk of child obesity,
An Xbox? – a necessity!
Just think how less obsessed we'd be,
With simple Elasticity.

The girls said it was simplicity,
The boys would say implicitly,
It didn't need electricity,
To join in Elasticity.

A five-foot gap from you to me,
We'd attach behind each knee,
Then adjust as necessary,
Our ankles joined elastically.

No branding would you need to see,
No need for any batteries,
Just play the game – quite simply,
Keep fit with Elasticity.

The line gets higher immediately,
As players jump the lines they see,
Losers swop with you or me,
To continue Elasticity.

Limbs get stretched – but properly,
Hearts are tested physically,
We're burning up the calories,
Just using Elasticity.

Fan-Gas-Tic

Le Petomane was a French name,
For a famous star of old,
He had the skill to fart at will,
Which made his crock of gold.

I think he had relations with someone from our nation,
As when I was at school,
I shared a class with one who'd pass,
A lot more than the rule.

His name was Vic his party trick would happen in assembly,
At "let us pray" he'd break away,
And cause a mini frenzy.

For the boy's part we admired his art,
The girls seemed less impressed,
The teachers would ignore it,
As they classed it as a test.

They didn't know who dealt the blow,
So, Vic just carried on,
When silence reigned, you'd see him strain,
Pandemonium!

Now Vic was proud he was so loud,
The kids knew it was him,
But he got his comeuppance,
Just before a morning hymn.

When silence fell, we all could tell,
What was coming next,
We watched for signs of Vic's behind,
His muscles being flexed,

But what was that a rat-a-tat,
From nowhere near to Vic,
A girl called Ann had trumped our man,
With something rather slick.

We fell about and let Vic pout,
It's seemed he'd met his match,
Ann now was queen, high in esteem,
For what she'd just let out.

From that day on his crown was gone,
To someone feminine,
Events like ours, not burning bras,
Is where equality began.

I Never Heard the Car...

I never heard the car,
Its Michelin tyres on the surface beneath,
The BMC motor that powered the beast,
The whine of the gears when selected for speed,
I never heard the car.

I didn't see the car,
Its four-pillared dome fronted with chrome,
Its driver relaxed as he headed for home,
Sun visor down and the radio on,
I didn't see the car.

Suddenly I felt the car,
I stepped from the gap 'tween bonnet and back,
A screech from the side stopped me dead in my tracks,
Chrome met with skin which gave with a crack,
Suddenly I felt the car.

Then I could smell the car,
Tyre tread fumes, a hint of the fuel,
Underseal smears on my jumper from school,
Cigarette smoke as the door opened full,
Then I could smell the car.

Then I feared the car,
Everything grazed confused – was I dead?
Multiple fracture the ambulancemen said,
Reliving again in my hospital bed,
Then I feared the car.

Teacher's Pet

To help develop an infant's mind,
We kept a little pet,
We got to choose a certain kind,
By vote, for what we'd get.

The timing wasn't set in stone,
It varied year to year,
It totally depended on,
When the last one disappeared.

We started with a gerbil,
A rat and then a mouse,
But most mums got quite verbal,
When we took it to our house.

They said, "We just don't like the tails,
And all their nasty habits,
Why don't you keep some ants or snails,
Or a little lop-eared rabbit?"

A hamster was then settled on,
The voting was a landslide,
The cage was cleaned and set for one,
And then we found the downside.

We'd watch and wait throughout the day,
Just looking for some movement,
We thought it had just passed away,
With no hope for improvement.

What none of us had thought about,
(And no one put us right),
Was hamsters just will not come out,
Until it's late at night!

Jack & Phil

Jack and Phil went up to Bill,
And tipped his cup of water,
Bill told Al (and Mike his pal),
And said there'd be a slaughter.

Al told Phil he bore no ill,
But Jack was going to cop it,
Bill pushed first before Miss Hurst,
Boomed out for Bill to "Stop it!".

Bill was wet, let's not forget,
And now he'd been admonished,
He turned to Al (without Al's pal),
And looked somewhat astonished.

Bill said to Steven let's get even,
This is down to Phil and Jack,
So, Al and Mike found both their bikes,
And stole them from the rack…

Contents of a Small Boy's Satchel

End of term would initiate a regular routine,
With everybody's satchel subject to a thorough clean,
They all had grown in volume and proportionately in weight,
And subjected to all weathers were in a somewhat sorry state.

The opening ceremony was a sure sight to behold,
A mother's eyes grew twice their size as the satchel did unfold,
The quantity of content would defy the laws of physics,
Did Dr Who leave this from an interplanetary visit?

It wasn't just the quantity that made a mother sigh,
The variety of goods crammed in was what really caught the eye.
And something else was not quite right, detected by the nostril,
Had something in there mummified or turned into a fossil?

This now called for serious kit before she took the plunge,
Experience said, "arm yourself! You cannot simply lunge",
So back into the kitchen to retrieve the tools required,
A trusty pair of Marigolds – immediately acquired.

As if it was a ticking bomb the contents were unpacked,
Arm's length action, finger, thumb would keep poor mum intact,
"I'm going in" ran through her mind – the no way back decision,
An exercise like this demanded military precision.

One by one the contents left their once nomadic home,
Distributed carefully for fear they may explode,
An exercise like this could not be undertaken lightly,
A note to self, made mentally to do this damn task nightly.

"How does he fit so much stuff in?" she'd think and shake her head,
"Another hour I won't get back, I should be in my bed!",
But finally, when the satchel's floor was clear for all to see,
She leant back, mopped her brow, and whispered, "Now inventory!"

Inventory of a Small Boy's Satchel

One school jumper, navy blue,
Compass from a Wayfinders shoe,
Marbles (small),
Marble (large),
Coupon from a block of marg,
Sandwich bag (no longer full),
Inside of a toilet roll,
Catapult with rubber grip,
Part of an Airfix battleship,
Plastic soldier (colour green),
Multicoloured plasticine,
One left pump (right one missing),
Letter from a girl (with kisses),
Corned beef sandwich (3 weeks old),
Putrid smell and green with mould,
Dandy and Beano comic books,
Fishing line, some floats, and hooks,
Homework sheet devoid of answers,
Picture of some belly dancers,
A tennis ball and half a fag,
Several toys from lucky bags,
Last of, but by no means least,
The remnants of a midnight feast!

Half-Term

It's 3:35 – a silent class,
Everybody gone at last,
For fourteen days, two week's refrain,
Before the mayhem starts again,
Empty hallways, floors to seal,
Echoes from the caretaker's heel,
Doors to wipe and walls to fill,
Victims of the overspill,
Panes are measured corner to corner,
And added to the glazier's order,
Lighting checked for faulty switches,
Bulbs replaced where there were hitches,
Tins of matt & tins of gloss,
To cover scratches or emboss,
Wooden floors with traffic wear,
In desperate need of repair,
Staffroom carpet got replaced,
A treat for teacher's secret space,
Notice boards to be reviewed,
Old signs and drawing pins removed,
Stationery cupboards checked for stock,
Pencils, paper, exercise books,
Teacher's tables left like shrines,
Reminders of what we'd left behind,
As if to say we're just on pause,
Until we walk back through the doors.

Lost Property

Where's your? – just fill in the blanks,
(A phrase you'd hear throughout the year),
Have you left it at the Baths?
(Check the latest destination, don't resort to desperation),
Did you leave it on your desk?
(Hardly likely, chairs on them nightly),
We haven't any time to mess,
What about at Amy's house?
(Call her mum, she's *your* best chum!),
Did you check when you came out?
How about the Cloakroom then?
(Didn't even bring a coat, as chances go that one's remote),
You will have been there just gone ten,
You sure you have not lied to me?
(It's disappeared, that fact is clear!),
Then you'd better search lost property!
(Oh no the very last resort, the saddest place for all things bought).

He-Said-She-Said

"I'm sorry Miss" said my friend Mike,
(Going for the pre-emptive strike),
"I haven't got my homework paper,
If that's ok, I'll hand in later?"

"What happened?" said Miss, slightly shocked,
Folding arms across her frock,
"What exactly made it late?"
"Would you care to elaborate?"

"Well," said Mike inhaling sharply,
Brain was ticking, thinking smartly,
"It wasn't just a simple act,
I'll try to keep it to the facts".

"I'm glad to hear that Michael dear,"
Said Miss, who bent and cocked an ear,
"Please inform me and the class,
Exactly just what came to pass."

"Well – I turned my back for just a moment,
Looked again and it was stolen,
The dog was heading for the door,
With something held within his jaw,
Before I could try and get it back,
He took off after next door's cat!"

"He dropped the paper on the road,
And as I know the Highway Code,
I looked both ways and then once more,
Only to see the paper soar,
Into the air to a garden beyond,
Where it landed in a goldfish pond."

"I fished it out but when I checked it,
The ink had run (as I'd expected),
Still, the thought of failing made me cry,
So, I put it on the hearth to dry."

"But just as I thought there could be no more,
My brother opened the living room door,
And whilst I lunged with all I'd in me,
It disappeared right up the chimney!"

Mike stopped and took a well-earned breather,
Smiled at Miss – surely a believer,
Miss stood up and straightened frock,
Glanced over her shoulder at the clock.

"Thank you Michael – fascinating!
Ten out of ten for being creative,
But while I've time let's check the facts,
Just to see how you'll react."

"Firstly, have you just bought a pet?
As your mum said you'd had none yet,
And unless I'm very much mistaken,
Your sister will be feeling shaken."

"Isn't she still your only sibling?
Now tell me Michael are you fibbing?
I think you are, and I know I'm right,
As I didn't set any homework last night!"

Confiscation

A treasure trove – Aladdin's Cave,
A box of Christmas presents saved!
Forbidden fruit, a burglar's loot,
A fix that any child would crave.

Full of wonder full of splendour,
Illicit goods from many spenders,
Those who'd dared had sneaked in there,
Was anything returned to sender?

What would stock the house of joy?
Who provided – girls or boys?
Did it stay or get away?
For owners once more to enjoy.

Exactly what was hoarded there?
Locked away beneath the stairs,
Out of reach by those who teach,
Oh, so close for those aware.

It was a time box – multi-storeyed,
Years of objects all told stories,
Loved when parted, now discarded,
All they had was former glory.

Kathy Won't Be In Today

I'm sorry Mr Jennings said the note.

She was looking forward to netball practice again but hasn't got over a bad cold.

She will be in tomorrow all being well...

I'm sorry Mr Jennings, the bruised knee Kathy got during practice on Monday is pretty swollen.

She will be in by Thursday all being well...

I'm sorry Mr Jennings, Kathy won't be able to play on Thursday.

She can't seem to shake this cold.

We have a doctor's appointment at 4pm.

She should be in next Monday...

I'm sorry Mr Jennings, Kathy has a hospital appointment next Thursday.

She won't be able to play netball for the next few weeks, doctor's orders you understand.

Will contact you when we know what is happening...

I'm sorry Mr Jennings, Kathy will need hospital treatment and will need to stay off for a few weeks.

Can you tell the class thank you for all their kind messages and cards,

It really helps to keep her spirits up while she's having the treatment...

Thank you, Mr Jennings, for all your class's kind words & condolences.

Please tell them that from me.

I'm sure you'll find the right words to let them all know why she won't be in...

My Goal

At nine years old my only goal was playing for the 'Alex,
I could head the ball,
Was very tall,
And showed a certain prowess.

I played my part at centre half,
And very few players got past,
Then one school game someone asked my name,
A breakthrough time at last?

The stepping stone along this road,
Was playing for the town,
The training day was Saturday,
Would it ever come around?

That it did, and with sparkling kit,
A squad of thirty met,
We split in groups – put through the hoops,
Until we all were spent.

Then came the crunch at Wednesday lunch,
The final eighteen cut,
A letter to say (from Cheshire FA),
Thanks for attending – but…

We've made our choice of eighteen boys,
You all showed great quality,
But others were better – etcetera, etcetera,
Sincerely – the committee.

The killer blow – what did they know?
Was exactly how it landed,
A dream in tatters – target shattered,
I'd done what they demanded!

Not good enough – the words felt rough,
But then again on reflection,
It's part of life – & no real strife
Was born of that rejection.

Handstands

When weather was dry and quite warm,
You'd see all the older girls swarm,
To the big playground wall,
Where the brickwork was tall,
And an orderly queue they would form.

Their teamwork was ever so slick,
As their teams seemed invisibly picked,
Arranged by their height,
With the ones that were slight,
At the back of each team (was that fixed?).

We shouldn't have needed to ask,
As they readied themselves for the task,
Cardies discarded,
Hair tied up and parted,
Readied for what always came last.

You see multiple handstands were planned,
With each team using the wall as a stand,
With the tallest going first,
Just like they'd rehearsed,
With the smallest the last of the band.

The boys watched the spectacle form,
As dresses were girls' uniform,
So, standing on hands,
Even immaculately planned,
Would give them all reason to scorn.

But girls are far brighter than them,
And as one they grabbed hold of each hem,
They couldn't have gone quicker,
As into their knickers,
Their dresses were tucked there and then!

An assortment of gingham pantaloons,
Girls looking at boys (the buffoons),
Then each girl upended,
As originally intended,
No wardrobe malfunctions to view.

LSD (aka Pounds Shillings and Pence)

It always was a mystery,
How it got christened LSD,
As when we used it actually,
It was pounds and pence to you and me.

Forget the tens and hundreds too,
We spent by a different rule,
A base of twelve was what we used,
It served us well through primary school.

There's no panache with decimalisation,
It's boring where's the specialisation?
"It's all about standardisation",
(Or dumbing down like other nations)

Words like "Half a Crown" or Florin,
We now regard as something foreign,
"Twenty pee" just sounds so boring,
Through the change our prices soaring.

A tanner or a thrupenny bit,
Had history all over it,
Now everyone would have a fit,
If Christmas pud had coins in it.

Redundant words like "Bob a Job",
Half a pound was called ten bob,
Twelve old pence a Shillings shop!!
Then 1971 – all stop.

Coincidence? – I think no way,
The day after Valentine's Day!
The shops had made sure they'd got paid,
All couples and government plans best laid.

School Trip

There was no school-owned minibus to ferry us about,
There wasn't any point in one, we just weren't taken out,
Apart from end of term time, and we would not object,
When teachers announced, "School Trip", and no-one would suspect…
… That the real reason for them, was sometimes a reward,
But other times I think you'll find, it stopped us getting bored,
With all the exams over, but two weeks from the break,
A project would be conjured up, if just for sanity's sake.

To notify all parents of the forthcoming event,
Each child was given a paper, on what needed to be spent,
"Dear parent" it began with, then details of the trip,
And ended "send deposit with the signed up torn off strip",
In those days very rarely, did anyone not pay,
The few that couldn't afford it, joined another class for the day,
That left an excited 20-odd with something to discuss,
Counting down the days to riding in Dolly Barrett's bus!

Now that was an experience I never will forget,
When the "Barrett's Bomb" drew up outside the primary school gate,
Just one door at the very front on a simple manual slide,
Was opened amid clouds of smoke from an always lit Park Drive,
Her hair was almost glacial white, with a very pale complexion,
The lipstick must have come straight from a "red is red" selection!
But take us all both there and back she always did with skill,
Knowing at least one of us would end up being ill…

Frogspawn

In spring when it started to warm,
Young boys would collect in a swarm,
They'd travel from far,
On a bike, with a jar,
To a pond where they knew there was frogspawn.

It was strange-looking stuff I admit,
And we messed up our clothes quite a bit,
Trying hard not to fall,
In the water at all,
As our mothers would have a blue fit.

Gallons of spawn were collected,
Held skywards and duly inspected,
Then the swarm would disband,
Nature's treasure in hand,
With plans to keep it undetected.

Some made it to little girls' chairs,
The inkwells or parts of the stairs,
A tiny proportion,
(More luck than good fortune),
Came legally into school care.

A goldfish bowl somehow appeared,
A home for our frogs to be reared,
We all watched and waited,
As tadpoles were created,
From the dots in the jelly girls feared.

But as the amphibians grew,
Time was running out and we knew,
That before they could jump,
The bowls contents were dumped,
In the pond we'd originally used!

Eleven-Plus

We played by Butler's rules,
A tripartite system fair to all,
Are you a boy or girl who will be eleven?
In the last year of primary school?
If yes, then go to next verse.

The three Rs – that's the key,
Just a single test to differentiate,
Between the Thinkers, The Doers and The Rest – simple,
Are you 11 this year?
If yes, then go to next verse.

Pass or fail – it all comes down to this,
Blend for seven years then segregate,
Tear down what you built for the price of a different coloured blazer,
Are you ready for this?
It doesn't matter, go to next verse.

Are you a boy or girl? Place your bets,
Are you rich or poor? Place your bets,
Are you mature enough? Place your bets…
…But remember the odds are stacked,
Just go to next verse.

You can't put a quart into a pint pot,

Spillage is failure in the grammatical sense,

Are you in the pint pot?

Perhaps you are the cream?

If you're not, and you're eleven this year – then just go...

Class Sharpener

A 1960's product every schoolroom used to host,
The single classroom entity that children used the most,
I'll make your pencil work again was all that it could boast,
Wood and lead were all it had to feed its little throat.

A portly alloy body with a handle on the right,
Standard stock and issue from a preferred Home Office site,
A feat of engineering lay silently inside,
To turn the bluntest pencil into an instrument to write.

It always did just what was asked, I never saw it fail,
Dispensing of its shavings in a tidy little bail,
No loss of electricity would make its services curtail,
Keyboards, icons, mice & apps weren't ready to prevail.

I've no idea where they all went or where you now might see them,
There isn't any reference to a sharpener museum,
The unsung metal heroes that once had millions feed them,
Despatched to sharpener heaven by an app that now has freed them.

Blue Peter Badge

I never got a Blue Peter Badge,
Although I did apply,
The same was true for all my friends,
Not even a reply!

Perhaps our work wasn't up to scratch,
Perhaps they were overwhelmed,
With paper mâché models,
Of imaginary friends.

We'd Uhu glue a carton or two,
Our ideas we thought fantastic,
Perhaps it was our failure to find,
That elusive sticky-back plastic.

But nonetheless we soldiered on,
Grey matter never dampened,
We eagerly waited for plans returned,
In the envelopes we'd stamped on.

Le pièce de résistance undoubtedly,
as the tinselled Advent Crown,
Which left many a wardrobe,
With clothing fallen down.

The ubiquitous coat hanger,
(The wire variety),
Was the sought after item,
Before Monday evening tea.

You only needed two of them,
Plus tinsel and some candles,
John Noakes and Valerie Singleton,
Explained how it was handled.

So almost every British house,
With children under ten,
Would celebrate each Christmas,
With a fire risk within!

We never lit the candles though,
No houses turned to ashes,
As being only nine or so
We had no need for matches!

Puddles

Take sunken tarmac & mislaid slabs,
A shower or two and what do you have?
Something no child could resist,
A source of infant interest.

It tempts the feet however booted,
To test for depth and if so suited,
To paddle, stomp with all your mates,
Before the thing evaporates.

A skilful jump from those who'd try,
Could splatter any passer-by,
Which usually caused squeals & shrieks,
As splashes hit their legs and cheeks.

But this was only short-lived fun
As the caretakers brush or the power of the sun
Would erase the culprit on the ground,
Until the next time showers abound.

That's Entertainment

No Netflix, Sky, or social media,
No World Wide Web to always feed you,
Radio was the main provider,
For everyone including minors.
"Are you sitting comfortably?
Then I'll begin" we'd hear with glee.
For under-fives, their daily slice.
Fifteen minutes quiet as mice.

When school had finished for the night,
We'd "Watch with Mother" in black and white,
Another fifteen-minute break,
"At last", the cry, "for sanity's sake",
No YouTube likes or Influencers,
No interactive video mentors,
Just simple mental stimulation,
Identical across the nation.

The same was true for adults too,
Sandwiched round the daily news,
Your choice was simple binary,
Commercials, or the BBC?
No Channel Four or Five as yet,
No surfing on the Internet,
No more from midnight that's your lot,
They'd switch it off and watch the spot…

 Matador

For exclusive discounts on Matador titles,
sign up to our occasional newsletter at
troubador.co.uk/bookshop